THE HEINLE READING LIBRARY

Academic Content Collection

Life in a
Cave

Toney Allman

THOMSON
*
™
HEINLE

Australia • Canada • Mexico • Singapore • United Kingdom • United States

For more information, contact
Thomson Heinle
25 Thomson Place
Boston, MA 02210 USA
Or you can visit our Internet site at elt.thomson.com

ISBN 1-4240-0265-6
Library of Congress Number: 2005910957

Printed in China

Contents

Chapter 1

The World of the Cave

The earth is a moving, changing planet. Earthquakes have buckled the earth's crust. Volcanoes have erupted. Oceans have covered the earth and then ebbed away. The plates of the earth have slid and moved continents. In ages past, great beds of firm rock called limestone formed under oceans out of the shells and bones of billions of ancient creatures. As the earth heaved and oceans receded, the limestone beds were forced upward and became mountains and rocky surfaces all around the world.

How Caves Grow

The water table, which stores the earth's fresh water underground, moved slowly through these limestone beds. Rain and streams ran over and through the limestone. Moving water, even a drop at a time, can be a tremendous force. The water, mixing with leaves and soil, becomes acid enough to dissolve cracks and holes, bit by bit, in the limestone. Over thousands of years, cracks and channels in the limestone became caves, passages, and shafts under the

A woman marvels at the beautiful features of a cave in Carlsbad Caverns, New Mexico.

Cross Section of a Cave System

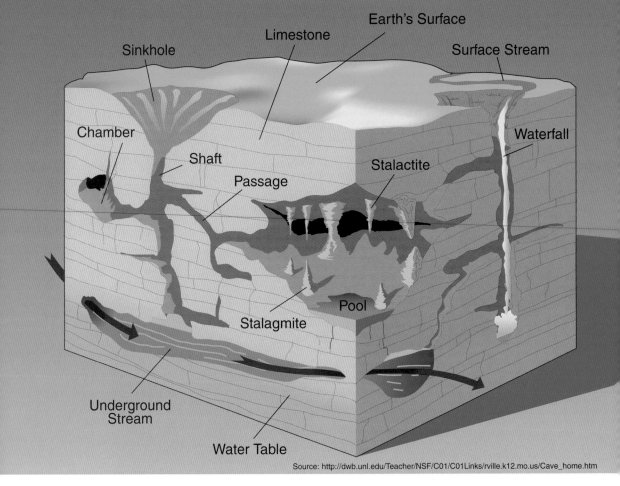

Sinkhole

Limestone

Earth's Surface

Surface Stream

Chamber

Waterfall

Shaft

Stalactite

Passage

Stalagmite

Pool

Underground
Stream

Water Table

Source: http://dwb.unl.edu/Teacher/NSF/C01/C01Links/rville.k12.mo.us/Cave_home.htm

earth's surface. Some of the caves are small. Some of the caves are as huge as many football fields. Other caves are connected by tunnels and passages to form cave systems many miles long.

Another world exists under the surface of the earth. Caves with great rooms and tunnels have formed within the rocks. Rivers run along for miles, sometimes appearing on the earth's surface and then abruptly disappearing underground. Some underground caves are filled with water. Other caves are shallow, dry, and dusty. The typical limestone cave, however, is livable space that extends deep into the earth. Lakes and pools form in depressions in the cave floor. Beautiful rock formations called **stalactites** hang like icicles from the ceiling. Domed **stalagmites** rise from the floor as water sinks into the earth and drips through the minerals in the cave roof. Weird shapes decorate the walls where water seeps into the cave. Other rock shapes form from the rivers and streams that run through the cave. Some rivers are so large that people navigate through the caves in inflatable boats.

Cave Entrances

Entrances to caves are sometimes open on the earth's surface. Doorways break in the sides of limestone hills or mountains. Some of these entrances are huge enough to dwarf a person standing inside. Others are insignificant clefts in the rock. Sinkholes or pits appear where the roof of a cave has collapsed or streams disappear underground. Some sinkholes can be as deep as the Empire State Building is tall. Wherever doorways to these underground worlds exist, living things move into the caves. Over time, the creatures of the caves evolve into a unique **ecosystem** that depends on the caves for survival.

Cave Zones

Cave ecosystems are complicated because conditions in the cave change the farther from the entrance one moves. The different areas of the cave

A hiker stands in the twilight zone of an enormous cave in Mexico.

are called zones, and different life exists in different zones. Still, all the life of the cave is dependent on other life within the cave and on the stable environment of the cave itself.

The first zone of the cave is the **twilight zone**. It extends from the entranceway as far back into the cave as light can reach. From the entrance, some sunlight comes into the cave. Depending on the size of the entrance, the sunlight may penetrate just a few feet or up to several hundred feet into the gloom of the cave. Even though it is dark compared to the outside surface, the small amount of light reaching into the cave makes vision possible in this zone. This area of the cave is affected by conditions outside, so the temperature outside the cave affects the twilight zone, too. Although it remains cooler in summer and warmer in winter than the surface, temperatures in the twilight zone change with the outside seasons.

The Dark Zone

Deeper into the cave is the area where light never penetrates. This is the **dark zone** of the cave. It is the blackest area on earth. The cave is black, cool, and wet. Nothing dries the water that drips through the ceiling and walls. No sunlight warms the cave. The cave takes on the temperature of the surrounding rocks. In the first part of the dark zone, the **variable-temperature zone**, temperatures in the air can vary a few degrees with the seasons outside

Twilight Zone

This zone extends from the cave's entrance to as far into the cave as sunlight can reach.

Dark Zone

This zone is deep inside the cave, where sunlight never reaches. (These photographs were taken using a flash camera.)

Variable-Temperature Zone

In this part of the dark zone, temperatures vary slightly with the seasons.

Constant-Temperature Zone

In the farthest reaches of the dark zone, the temperature stays the same year-round.

the cave. Any stream in the zone, however, stays the same temperature all year long.

Deeper into the cave, the **constant-temperature zone** has temperatures in water and air that never change. This zone continues as far as the cave does. The rocks of the cave remain the same temperature as the average yearly temperature on the outside surface. In Kentucky caves, for instance, the temperature in the constant-temperature zone remains about 56 degrees Fahrenheit (13.3 degrees Celsius) all year long.

A cave can be a forbidding place for animals. Not many creatures can tolerate cold, wet darkness all the time. Finding food to eat can be very hard in the endless night. Where sunlight never penetrates, no green plants can grow. On the earth's surface, animals and people could not survive without green plants. Yet, some living things manage to make homes in caves.

Troglos Means Cave

Cave visitors, cave lovers, and cave dwellers all use caves in different ways and for different reasons. Cave visitors are the animals that live on the earth's surface but come into caves to find food, safety, or homes. These cave animals are called **trogloxenes**. Trogloxenes do not live permanently in a cave but come and go. Bats, some birds, pack rats, raccoons, and snakes are examples of cave visitors or trogloxenes.

Troglophiles are the cave lovers. These are animals that can spend their whole lives in a cave but could survive in other dark, damp environments if they had to. Cave crickets, earthworms, and some beetles and salamanders are examples of troglophiles.

Troglobites are cave dwellers. These creatures are trapped in the perpetual darkness of the cave, for they can exist nowhere else, not even in the cave's twilight zone. They depend on the unchanging constant-temperature zone for survival and are some of the strangest animals on earth. No mammals are cave dwellers, as none can survive the harsh conditions of the dark zones. Troglobites are more primitive animals such as fish, salamanders, and spiders. All troglobites are completely blind. Many do not even have eyes. Most troglobites have no color or are ghostly white.

Visitors, Lovers, and Dwellers Together

Cave dwellers live in a difficult environment, always close to starvation. Their populations in each cave are small because there is so little food in the dark zone of the cave. They must depend on the cave visitors and cave lovers to bring food into their homes. They must be able to eat almost anything that washes into the cave in underground streams or rivers. Amazingly, troglobites have survived very well for thousands of years because of the successful ecosystem of the cave.

Cave Animals

Trogloxenes

These are the cave visitors. They enter the cave seeking food, shelter, or safety.

Raccoon

Bat

Rattlesnake

Troglophiles

These are the cave lovers. They thrive in the cave's dark, damp environment but could survive in other, similar environments.

Earthworm

River Shrimp

Troglobites

These are the cave dwellers. They never leave the darkest part of the cave.

Cave Crayfish

Blind Cave Crab

Most trogloxenes and troglophiles prefer the more comfortable environment of the twilight zone to the dark zones. Food is easier to find, they can see where they are going, and they can move outside to the surface when necessary. A few cave visitors and cave lovers, however, are comfortable in the dark zone. The story of how they interact with the cave dwellers is a miracle of nature in a unique and fascinating environment.

Chapter 2

Keystones of the Cave

The few cave visitors and cave lovers that live in dark zones are **keystone species** of caves. Without them, no ecosystem would exist. Keystone creatures keep caves alive by bringing in food in a very surprising way.

Guano from the Keystones

Keystone species of cave ecosystems include bats, cave crickets, and unusual birds. The caves they inhabit are **guano** caves. Guano is droppings, or **feces**, from the keystone creatures. It is disgusting and smelly to people, but guano is rich and welcomed by the cave dwellers of the dark zone. Guano is food, brought into the cave from outside. Without it, the cave would starve.

A biologist (right) is knee-deep in guano, the droppings produced by bats roosting on the cave ceiling (above).

Many different kinds of bats are keystone species that bring food into caves. They live in large groups, called colonies, which can consist of millions of bats.

The Bats of Bracken Cave

The largest bat colony in the world lives in Bracken Cave in Texas. They are Mexican free-tailed bats. Twenty to 40 million live in Bracken Cave. Each spring, the bats fly to Bracken Cave from their winter homes in Mexico. During the day, they roost in the cave, hanging upside down and clinging to the ceiling and walls with the sharp claws of their hind feet. The bats are packed in thickly. In each square foot (0.3 square meter) of wall space, five hundred bats can hang, sleeping together and dropping guano on the cave floor.

The Guano Cave Floor

From the millions of bats, a constant rain of guano and urine falls. Fleas and ticks that fall off the bats as they clean themselves shower down to the floor and cave pools. Old, sick bats and weak, newborn pups lose their grip on the ceiling and crash down from above. The sickening surface, many feet deep in guano, is alive with a mass of troglobites that devour all the food. The cave dwellers eat ticks, fleas, and dead bat bodies, but most importantly, they eat the guano itself. Guano is nourishment for the cave.

The bats are able to provide all this nourishment because they are trogloxenes—able to leave the cave each night to feed. At dusk, whirlwinds of bats funnel out of the cave entrance to the surface. They fly in the night sky, feeding on insects. Each bat can eat more than half its body weight in insects each night. Two hundred tons (181 metric tons) of moths, mosquitoes, and other insects are swallowed nightly by the bats of Bracken Cave.

When daybreak approaches, all the bats fly home again. They swoop through the entrance and wend

At dusk millions of Mexican free-tailed bats fly out of Texas's Bracken Cave in search of food.

their way into the cave's dark zone, back to their day-time roosts. Even though it is completely black inside, the bats have no trouble finding their way.

Echolocation

Bats do not have to see in the cave to fly. Bats fly by using **echolocation**. While it is flying, a bat makes very high-pitched squeaks, too high for human ears to hear. The squeaks make sound waves that bounce off obstacles ahead. The sound waves echo off the obstacle and bounce back to the bat's very sensitive ears. The shape and size of the echoes tell the bat what is ahead. The bat can recognize a stalactite, a wall, and even another flying bat. With its echolocation system, a bat can swoop and turn quickly, avoiding every danger and flying safely into and out of the cave. On the surface, at night, the echolocation helps the bat catch insects in the air.

The Bat Nursery

The bats use the cave as a nursery to rear their young. Bat babies are called pups. They are born naked and helpless, able only to cling to the cave wall with their sharp little claws. All the pups roost together in a special area of the cave. They remain there each night while their mothers are outside feeding. Each day, every mother finds and nurses her own pup. Pups grow quickly. In about a month, they are furred, fat, and ready to fly. Then, they join

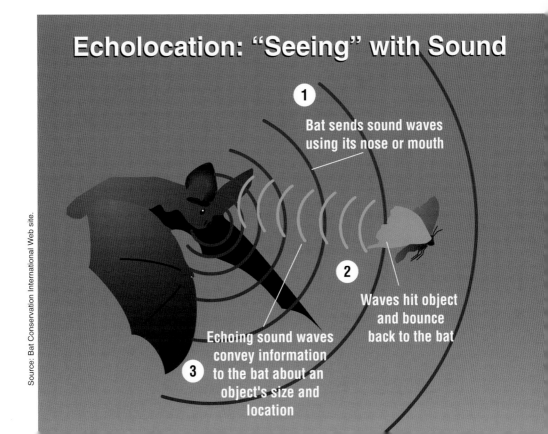

Echolocation: "Seeing" with Sound

1 Bat sends sound waves using its nose or mouth

2 Waves hit object and bounce back to the bat

3 Echoing sound waves convey information to the bat about an object's size and location

the other bats each night to hunt for insects. When cold weather comes, all the bats abandon their summer home and migrate back to Mexico.

Hibernating Bats

Most bats in the United States do not migrate to warmer places in the wintertime. They **hibernate** in the dark zones of caves. Gray bats, for example, gather in colonies in the fall and hibernate in only nine caves in Kentucky, Tennessee, Arkansas, Missouri, and Alabama. The bats go into the dark zones and hang from the ceilings and walls. They are fat from good summertime feeding. They go into a deep sleep in which all their body functions slow down. Their body temperatures drop, their heartbeats slow, and they take so few breaths that they look almost dead.

All winter, the bats sleep. The constant temperature and isolation in the cave protect them. If a hibernating bat is disturbed, it is in terrible danger. Waking up uses energy and stored fat. A bat that wakes up may die of starvation before spring comes with its insect food. Undisturbed caves mean survival for hibernating bats.

Oilbirds in Guacharo Cave

Bats are not the only trogloxenes that are keystone species in caves. In Venezuela's Guacharo Cave lives the oilbird, a trogloxene that is one of the strangest birds on earth. The oilbird can be almost 2 feet (0.6

meters) long. It has a 3-foot (0.9-meter) wingspan and huge eyes that help it to see food at night. The oilbird does not use its eyes in the cave, though. It depends on echolocation, just as the bats do.

Oilbirds live in caves all year round. They roost and raise young inside the cave. Each night, the oilbirds fly out of the cave to the surface to feed on seeds and fruits. At dawn, they return to their dark-zone homes, where oilbird guano falls to the floor and supports a whole community of troglobites.

Oilbirds roost in caves during the day and fly out at night to feed on seeds and fruits.

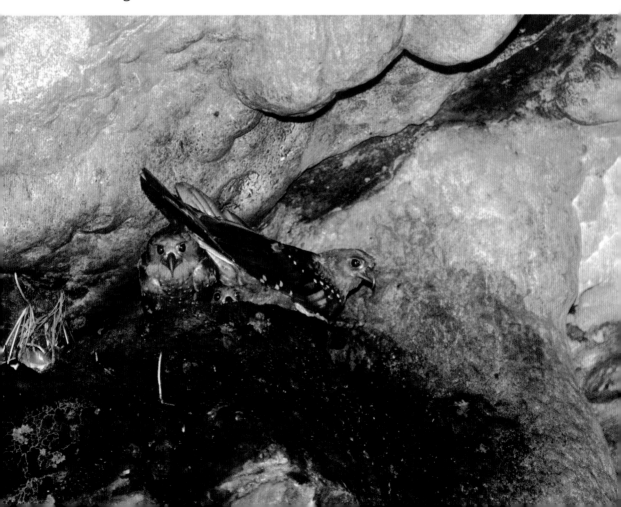

Cave Crickets in Cathedral Cave

Troglophiles can be keystone species, too. In Cathedral Cave in Kentucky lives a community of about thirty-seven hundred cave crickets. These crickets look different from crickets on the surface. Their bodies are paler, their eyes smaller, and their antennae longer than those of surface crickets. With their longer feelers, cave crickets are able to discover food in the darkness more easily. Cave crickets are scavengers, eating dead little bits of almost anything, animal or plant. Some food is available in the cave itself, but cave crickets also go outside on the surface for food. Strangely, they do not chirp outside at night as normal, surface crickets do.

A cave cricket uses its long feelers to find food in the darkness of a cave.

On summer nights, cave crickets take turns going outside for food. The first night, for example, one-third of the crickets go to the surface and spend the night feeding. They return to the cave at daybreak. The second night, another third of the crickets go out to feed. On the third night, the last of the crickets take their turns. Each group of crickets knows when it is their turn, but no one has been able to figure out how they know or why they take turns. The system works well for the crickets, though, and sustains a community of cave dwellers. Cricket guano accumulates only about .5 inches (1.3 centimeters) thick and so can support less life than bat guano. The thirty-seven hundred crickets in Cathedral Cave support about seven hundred cave dwellers.

All guano feeds a host of tiny animals. Other troglobites eat the animals that eat the guano. Because of the keystone species of the guano caves, many strange and wonderful cave dwellers populate the underground worlds.

Chapter 3

The Cave Dwellers

All the troglobites of the cave depend on guano to survive. Food is never plentiful in a cave ecosystem, but the troglobites cannot leave to search elsewhere for nourishment. The cave dwellers live only if the guano producers—the keystone species— remain alive and healthy in their caves.

Guano Eaters

Tiny cave-dwelling creatures crawl blindly on the guano cave floor and in the cave waters, searching for food. Isopods live in the cave pools or rivers. They are small crustaceans that look like little, many-legged bugs. They eat germs in the cave waters, decaying matter, and guano that falls into the pools. They are joined in their guano banquets by flies, beetles, millipedes, and other tiny insects. All are troglobites, white and blind, that eat anything they can find in order to survive.

Sometimes, the troglobites find the only plants that grow inside a cave. Molds, like the growth on old bread, are plants that get their energy from rotting matter instead of sunshine. Fungi, which are plants like mushrooms or the fuzzy growth on tree bark, can also grow in the dark. Both molds and fungi are able to grow in the dark zone because they do not need sunlight, as green plants do. They get the energy to grow from guano. The molds and fungi do not grow for long. They are quickly discovered and eaten by the starving troglobites.

Drifting on a small piece of wood, a blind, white isopod feeds on bits of decayed matter in a cave pool.

Cave flatworms float in pools or crawl on wet cave floors. These strange worms are about .5 inches (1.3 centimeters) long. They are white and eyeless. They move blindly along the cave floor, eating guano. Tiny, white cave insects join in the feast. As the cave flatworms crawl, they leave a slimy, sticky trail behind them. Sometimes, an insect crawls on this trail and gets stuck. The cave flatworm retraces its trail and gobbles up the stuck insect, too.

Cave Beetles

Cave beetles live on the cave floor, along with the flatworms. Cave beetles are pale and blind, just like other troglobites, but they have no trouble discovering food. They ravenously attack fungi, molds,

Beetles consume a dead bat lying in a pile of guano on a cave floor.

bat fleas and ticks, and guano. When a bat crashes to the cave floor, death is very quick. The beetles swarm over and cover the body, stripping it to the bones in minutes. The troglobite beetles in a bat guano cave eat anything they can find.

Amazingly, cave beetle babies do not eat at all. Unlike other beetles, cave beetles lay big eggs, with huge yolks to feed the developing babies. As soon as the cave beetles' eggs have hatched, the fat, well-fed young roll themselves into a bit of clay from the cave floor. The clay shell hardens and protects them as they grow. They grow to be mature beetles before they starve to death. Inside their clay balls, the young beetles are saved from trying to fight for food or being eaten in the harsh cave environment. Once they are adults, they are ready to roam the cave floor and battle the other cave dwellers for their meals.

Finding enough food in the cave is always a battle. The battle is especially difficult for predators that eat other animals in order to survive. Troglobite predators include spiders, crayfish, salamanders, and fish. They are the troglobites that eat the animals that eat the guano. Their lives are a constant effort to find enough food to stay alive.

Ozark Salamanders

In bat guano caves in Missouri, Oklahoma, and Arkansas live blind Ozark salamanders. These troglobite salamanders are born in water pools or streams within the cave. When an Ozark salamander is young, it looks very much like other salamanders. It is brown, chubby, and has small dark eyes. As the salamander grows to land-living adulthood, however, it loses the characteristics that are of no value in the dark zone. Its eyelids seal shut. Underneath the eyelids, the eyes waste away until only little bumps are left. Eyes are useless to the Ozark salamander in the unending blackness of the cave.

Suited to Darkness

Skin color has no value to the salamander either. A salamander's color protects it from the burning rays of the sun or helps it to hide among the plants on the surface. An Ozark salamander does not face these problems. Its brown color fades away. The salamander becomes pale and colorless until blood vessels and organs can be seen through its skin. Its body becomes long and thin. The Ozark salamander looks like a very helpless creature, but it is well suited to its life in the darkness.

Ozark salamanders develop vibration sensors all along the length of their bodies. These sensors feel the tiniest movements in the air or water. When another animal comes near the blind Ozark salamander, its presence is immediately felt by the vibration sensors on the salamander's body. The salamander can easily escape a predator or locate a prey animal and grab a meal. Blind Ozark salamanders eat flatworms, insects, isopods, or anything else they can find in the cave.

An Ozark salamander finds food in its cave by sensing vibrations with its body.

Blind Cave Fish

Another predator of the cave dark zone is the blind cave fish. It lives in underground streams and rivers and is only four or five inches (twelve centimeters) long. Like the Ozark salamander, it is completely blind. It has no eyes at all, just little bumps where eyes should be, and is a ghostly white. Being a predator in a dark-zone stream is not easy because there is so little to eat in the cave waters. Blind cave fish have to be able to eat almost anything, even bits of dead leaves that wash in from the surface. Even so, populations of cave fish in underground rivers are small.

Upper Twin Cave in Indiana, for example, is a big cave, measuring 4,500 feet (1,371.6 meters) long. Only

80 to 125 fish can live in its underground river. Each fish swims slowly in its own territory, conserving energy by not moving quickly. The blind cave fish uses the vibration sensors along the length of its body to sense the movement of prey or even the movement of drifting leaves from the surface. It also has a large head with many extra vibration sensors that feel the slightest disturbance in the water. It can actually identify the tiny movements of water fleas, which cannot even be seen without a microscope. The blind cave fish efficiently discovers anything that will make a meal. It eats isopods, flatworms, insects, and little, blind crayfish. If it finds baby cave fish, it

A blind cave fish searches for food along the bottom of a river in a cave in China.

will eat them, too. Blind cave fish are always close to starvation, but by moving slowly and eating almost anything, they are able to survive.

Blind cave fish in other caves survive by being even smaller than the fish in Upper Twin Cave. The River Styx, for example, runs through Mammoth Cave in Kentucky. The blind cave fish in the River Styx are only two inches (five centimeters) long. The smaller the fish, the less food it needs to stay alive.

On the Edge

Troglobite predators are small and few. There are just enough of them in each cave to maintain a stable ecosystem. Just enough predator troglobites eat just enough guano-eating troglobites that all the cave creatures can find food and survive.

Anything that affects the food supply, especially a loss of the guano, could wipe out most of the troglobites. Any change in the unending darkness or the constant temperature easily threatens their lives. Unfortunately, such changes have occurred over and over in the underground worlds. Human interference has often caused nature's delicately built system to crash.

Chapter 4

The Fragile Cave

Many human activities have transformed caves from living ecosystems to empty, lifeless shells. Tourism, pollution, and the persecution of bats have been especially devastating to the caves and the life within them.

Tourist Caves

When people discovered deep caves, they were enchanted by the marvels they found. Cave owners conducted tours for sightseers who wanted to experience the beauty of the rock formations. Mammoth Cave in Kentucky was opened to the public in 1838. Tourists took boat rides down the underground rivers. They found themselves in great cathedral-like rooms with

Rock Formations in Caves

Gypsum Flowers

Translucent Stalactites

Calcite Cave Pearls

Aragonite Soda Straw

stalactites, stalagmites, and stone flowers formed from a mineral called gypsum. They were amazed by snow-balls of rock growing on the walls. To make tourism easier, Mammoth Cave's owners built bridges and steps throughout the maze of rooms. They blasted with dynamite to enlarge the entrance and make trails through rock. Souvenir stands and brilliant lighting appeared.

In Carlsbad Caverns in New Mexico, tunnels were blasted through rock, too. Entrances were en-larged, and lunchrooms were added. By 1927 elec-tric lights replaced torches along paved trails through the cave system. Tourists flocked to the caves to see colorful draperies, pearls, flowers, and coiled ribbons, all made of stone.

Tourism was thrilling to sightseers, but for the caves, it was terribly destructive. Tourists broke off pieces of beautiful formations and took them home for souvenirs. Soot and dirt from smoky torches and oil lamps ruined the beauty of rock formations and prevented them from growing.

Tourists and the Ecosystem

As destructive as tourism was to the cave rocks, it was worse for the living creatures. People's activi-ties changed the ecosystem. Blasting through rock and enlarging entrances changed the temperature and air within the caves. Animals in the constant-temperature zone could not survive the altered con-ditions. If they could not retreat deeper into dark zones, they died. Noisy, disruptive people intruded in bat roosts, frightening and upsetting the bats. Bats could not even tolerate the breezes created by new passages. They abandoned their homes. The food they provided for the cave dwellers was gone. Whole ecosystems died from starvation.

Lights and lunchrooms did a large share of damage, too. In Carlsbad Caverns, for example, food served in the lunchroom enticed cockroaches and mice to enter the cave. Because they could see, these animals easily made homes there. Troglobites were either eaten or starved out by the animals that could find food more quickly.

Artificial lighting adds color to the stalactites and stalagmites of a cave in Carlsbad Caverns.

When tourists saw the troglobites, they were fascinated by such otherworldly creatures. They captured the cave dwellers and took them home for souvenirs. In some Kentucky and Indiana caves, so many cave fish were captured that the fish disappeared completely.

People were unaware of how much they damaged the caves when they explored and collected souvenirs. By the middle of the twentieth century, caves everywhere were being loved to death.

Reversing Damage

Today, people understand how fragile caves are. Governments and cave protection societies work to protect and restore caves whenever possible. Many

A group of tourists explores Kentucky's Mammoth Cave by boat in the early 1900s.

caves in the United States are now guarded by the National Parks System. The areas of these caves that are developed are still dead areas with little or no life, but sections of the caves remain wild and are carefully preserved by park managers.

Like other tourist caves, Carlsbad Caverns has almost no life in the tourist cave section. However, its Bat Cave is guarded and never opened to the public. The bats live in peace in this section of Carlsbad. The fragile ecosystem remains undisturbed. The cave life that depends on the bats' guano is protected. Since Carlsbad began protecting the Bat Cave ecosystem, the number of bats living there has risen from half a million to a million bats.

Carlsbad managers also improved conditions in the public parts of the cave. Garbage and food from the lunchroom are collected and removed each night. Even old wood, such as from torches used in the past, is being removed, since it is not a natural part of the ecosystem.

Pollution in Caves

Despite all the care that national parks take, caves can be damaged by people who never visit. People sometimes throw garbage down sinkholes or into cave entrances, causing deadly pollution of the caves. This happened in the Hidden River Cave in Kentucky. In 1916 tourists visited Hidden River and took boat rides to see the wonderful formations and blind cave fish. By the 1930s, however, the fish were all dead, and the cave smelled so bad that no one wanted to enter. The people who lived in the town by Hidden River Cave had been throwing their garbage down sinkholes. The sewage from the town was dumped into streams that led directly into the underground river. People had not understood how all their waterways were connected to the cave. They had not known that sinkholes fed into the cave. Hidden River became a dead cave.

In 1989 all pollution was finally stopped in Hidden River Cave. Luckily, the cave is part of a cave system, with the river flowing underground through miles of different caves. Today, troglobites are gradually returning to Hidden River from upstream caves. Tourists can visit the river again and see the blind cave fish.

Endangered Bats

Wherever people work to restore cave ecosystems, they are most successful when they educate the public to help protect the caves. Public education is especially important for bat protection. Bats suffer because people disturb them, kill them, or destroy their dark-zone homes, by accident and on purpose. Many different kinds of bats are endangered.

In the past, most countries used a powerful poison called DDT to kill harmful insects. Sadly, DDT also kills bats. The United States no longer uses DDT, but other countries still do. Bats suffer many deaths from this use of poison.

Below: A biologist examines the pesticide deliberately used to kill bats in a cave.

Above: To protect bat populations, wildlife managers place bat-friendly gates at cave entrances to keep people out.

Many more bats, however, are killed when their caves are disturbed. Thirty million Mexican free-tailed bats lived in Eagle Creek Cave in Arizona in 1963. By 1969 there were only thirty thousand. No one is positive what happened to the bats, but distressed citizens found hundreds of shotgun shells and spent rifle bullets in the cave entrance. Trespassers can devastate caves.

At Long Cave in Kentucky, managers erected a barrier to keep out trespassers. Mistakenly, it made entry too hard for the Indiana bats that lived there. In the 1940s fifty thousand bats lived in Long Cave.

By the 1990s fewer than eight hundred bats were left. Long Cave now has a bat-friendly gate. The gate has wide steel bars so that the bats can go in and out of the cave, but people cannot enter. Slowly, the bat population is increasing. A year after the new gate was put up, a hundred new bats were counted in the cave. Today, bat-friendly gates at cave entrances are successfully protecting bats around the world.

Bat Conservation International is a worldwide organization that values bats and fights to keep them safe. The organization bought Bracken Cave in Texas so that it could protect the bats. People are not allowed to enter the cave. The bats and cave ecosystem remain undisturbed. The tragedies of Long Cave and Eagle Creek Cave will not be repeated in Bracken Cave.

Save the Caves

The more people learn about bat caves and the needs of bats, the better they can protect this keystone species. Without bats, the world of the cave dwellers cannot survive. People who love bats, troglobites, and the beautiful caves are fighting today for the lives of cave ecosystems. They ask everyone to protect caves, fight pollution, and save the underground worlds for future generations.

Glossary

constant-temperature zone: The dark zone area of the cave where temperatures never change.

dark zone: The area of the cave where light never penetrates.

echolocation: The way a bat "sees" with its ears, by using reflected sounds to identify and locate objects.

ecosystem: The interconnected community of plants and animals that depend on one another in a specific pocket of nature.

feces: Bowel movements or wastes that are passed out of the body.

guano: Bat droppings or bowel movements.

hibernate: To spend the winter in a special kind of sleep in which body functions slow down and body temperature drops. The hibernating animal neither eats nor drinks, but survives on stored fat reserves.

keystone species: The animal that is especially important to the survival of the many other animals in an ecosystem.

stalactite: A limestone formation that looks like an icicle and hangs down from the ceiling of a cave.

stalagmite: A limestone formation that builds up

from the floor of a cave because of water dripping from above.

troglobite: An animal that is a cave dweller. It can live nowhere else but in the dark zone of a cave.

troglophile: An animal that is a cave lover. It can complete its life cycle in a cave, but also can leave the cave when necessary.

trogloxene: An animal that is a cave visitor. It does not live in the cave permanently, but comes and goes.

twilight zone: The area of the cave where enough light penetrates that human vision is possible.

variable-temperature zone: The area of the cave where air temperatures can change with the temperature outside the cave.

For Further Exploration

Books

Caroline Arnold, *Bat*. New York: Morrow Junior Books, 1996. The many photographs in this book illustrate the wonderful world of bats. The author describes bat history, bat lives, bat folk tales, and bat needs.

Laurence Pringle, *Bats! Strange and Wonderful*. Honesdale, PA: Caroline House, Boyds Mills Press, 2000. This easy-to-read book describes bats around the world, the way they live, and what valuable, fascinating creatures they are. See pictures of many different bats, even vampire bats!

Web Sites

BCI's "Bat Chat" Audiotape (www.batcon.org/discover/echo.html). Listen to the calls of different kinds of bats. The echolocation sounds have been made audible to human ears with a bat detector.

The Cave Life Page (http://wasg.iinet.net.au/clife.html). This page is dedicated to photographs of many cave animals. See insects, crayfish, bats, and other unusual creatures.

Echo the Bat: Images, NASA Science Education (http://imagers.gsfc.nasa.gov/index.html). Not all bats live in caves. Read the story of little Echo the bat and join him in his adventures.

KidZone Bats (www.kidzone.ws/animals/bats/index.htm). See images of many kinds of bats, learn fun bat facts, and play some bat games. This is a large site with many links to bat information.

The Virtual Cave (www.goodearthgraphics.com/virtcave.html). Go on a virtual cave exploration and discover a cave. Other kinds of caves exist besides limestone caves. This site explains cave formations from lava, sandstone, and in the sea. There are great pictures of different kinds of caves.

Index

Picture Credits

About the Author

Toney Allman holds degrees from Ohio State University and the University of Hawaii. She currently lives in Virginia, where she enjoys gardening, hiking, collecting antique bottles, and learning about the natural world.